HOW TO DRAW CUTE RABBITS CHIBI VERSION

Part 2

HAVE FUN LEARNING
STEP BY STEP HOW TO CREATE
BEAUTIFUL BUNNIES FROM A CIRCLE

MERÚ ILLUSTRATIONS

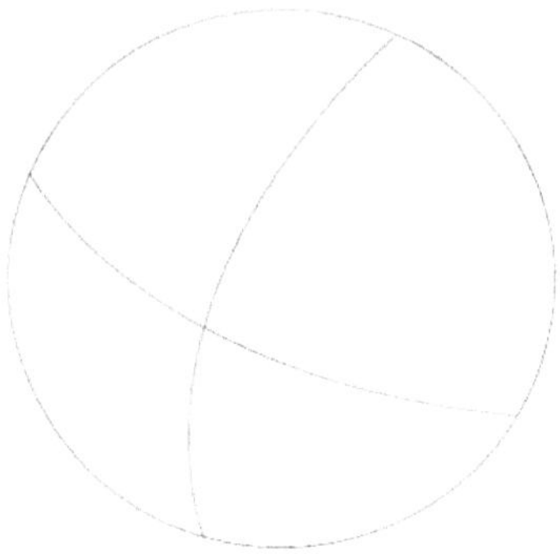

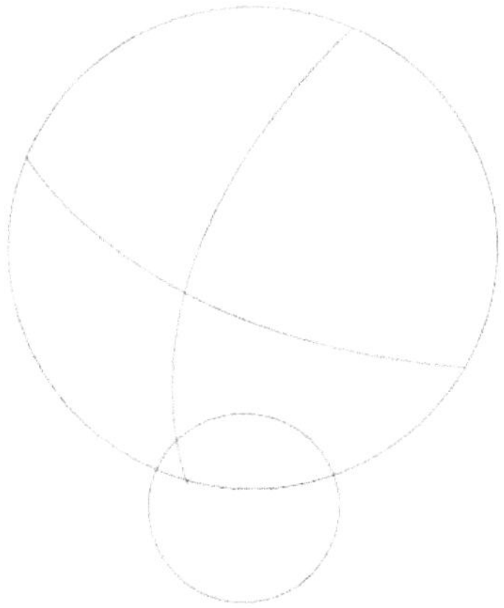

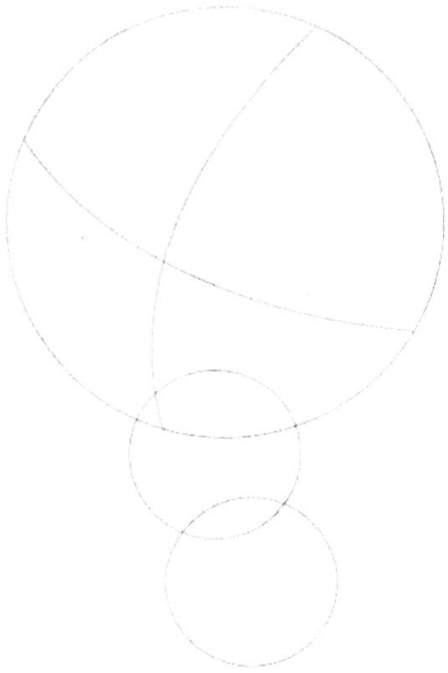

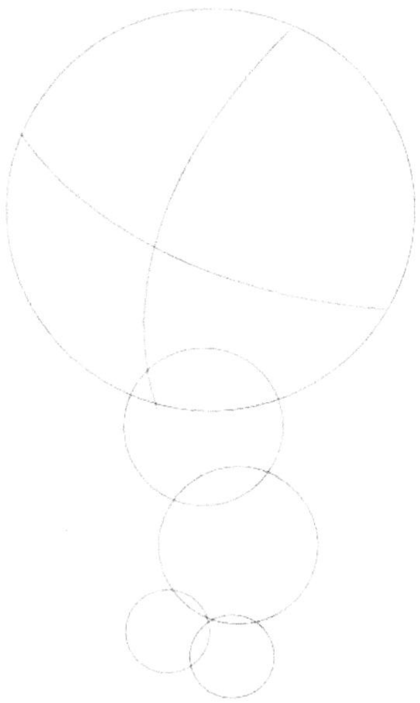

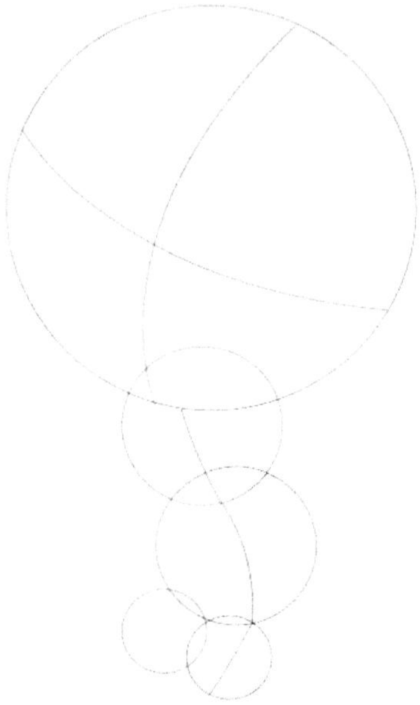

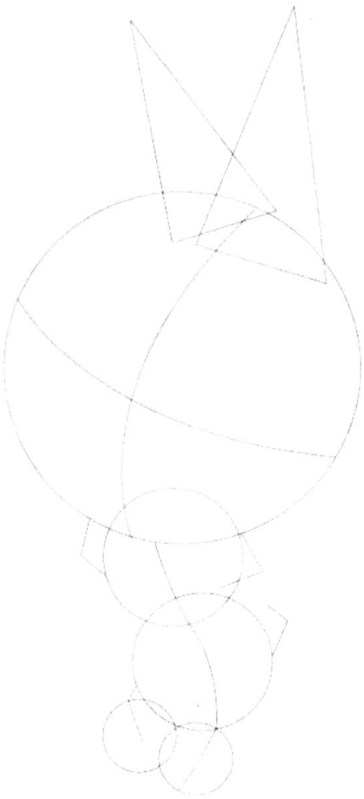

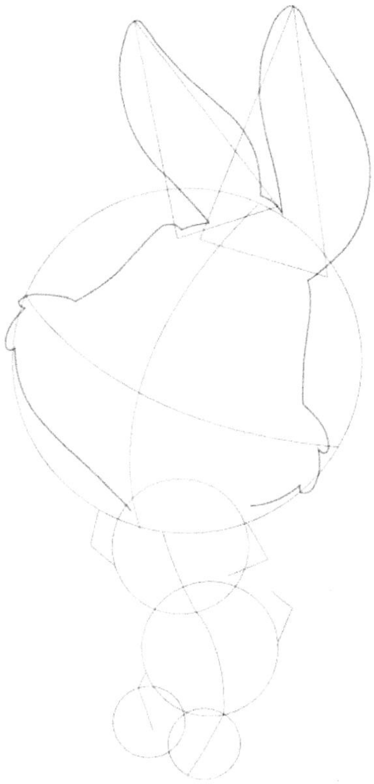

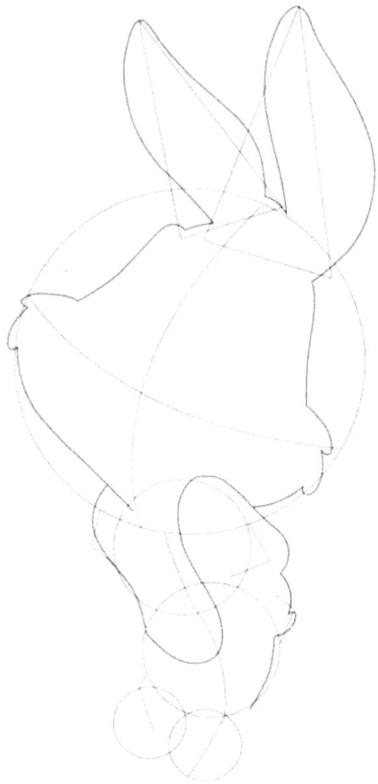

www.ingramcontent.com/pod-product-compliance
Lightning Source LLC
Chambersburg PA
CBHW050801290526
45792CB00008B/2280
* 9 7 8 1 0 8 9 3 2 0 4 9 4 *